W9-ARW-809

WRESTLING

About the authors

Arnold Umbach began a winning career in wrestling in 1919 when he wrestled as a prep under E.C. Gallager. He graduated from Southwestern College, and while there he was conference wrestling champion at 158 pounds from 1924-1927. He began a coaching career in 1929 that included twenty seven years as wrestling coach at Auburn University. During those years at Auburn, Coach Umbach's teams emassed an impressive 249-28-5 record. A past president of the National Wrestling Coaches Association, he has been honored by both the state legislature of Alabama and the City of Auburn.

Warren Johnson's wrestling background dates to 1938 when he began wrestling with the University of Denver. During the two-year period beginning in 1948 he was the head wrestling coach at Boston University. Currently a member of the Health Education and Physical Education department at the University of Maryland, Johnson has done extensive research on wrestling and wrestlers.

He is the author of numerous books in the areas of health and physical education, and he has also served on the planning committee for a White House Conference on Food, Nutrition, and Health.

EXPLORING SPORTS SERIES

WRESTLING

Arnold Umbach
Warren Johnson

wcb
Wm. C. Brown Publishers
Dubuque, Iowa

Cover photo by Bob Coyle

Consulting Editor

Aileene Lockhart
Texas Woman's University

Evaluation Materials Editor

Jane A. Mott
Texas Woman's University

Copyright © 1966, 1977, 1984 by Wm. C. Brown Company Publishers

Library of Congress Catalog Card Number: 84-070348

ISBN 0-697-00293-4

Printed in the United States of America

2   00293   01

Contents

Preface

This is the second edition of Wrestling. It provides the basic fundamentals of wrestling that a beginner should know.

Wrestling is a demanding sport requiring agility, endurance, flexibility, quickness, strength, and toughness. It is a great physical fitness builder of young men, and it is one of the fastest growing of sports.

This book has been greatly expanded in order to give the beginner a greater knowledge of the sport. Every important step in each maneuver is clearly shown in photographs. Thus, it is easy for the beginner to analyze each important step. The description and comments about each photograph explain the crucial points in each sequence.

Coaching points that should be stressed in making each maneuver successful have also been added to this book. The common mistakes are pointed out in order to show why maneuvers sometimes fail to work. This gives the wrestler a method to evaluate each maneuver.

Evaluation questions are included in each chapter. These questions afford the reader typical examples of the kind of understanding and level of skill that he should be acquiring as he moves toward proficiency in wrestling.

It is the sincere hope of the authors that the material in this book will serve to enrich the experience of young men who are interested in wrestling. The information in this book is clearly suitable and useful for beginning wrestlers of all ages.

This book was prepared with the assistance of a number of individuals. We are grateful to all who gave us their cooperation. Jeff Conway took all of the photographs and three members of the Auburn University Wrestling Team, Troy Downey, Ray Downey, and Gordon Nelson did the demonstrations of the wrestling maneuvers. To these men we say thank you.

History of wrestling

1

The history of most of our popular sports dates back only a few decades (basketball and American football) or possibly a few centuries (golf and tennis). Some modern sports, however, got their start long before recorded history. Wrestling is one of these very ancient sports that may have begun in the playful sense that cub bears, puppies, or children "tussle"—and/or in the combative sense of men struggling violently for survival—perhaps both. We can only guess at its origins as a "sport" in the remote past.

At any rate, we know that by the time of the ancient Egyptians and Greeks wrestling was a highly developed sport. That is, it was competitive; it had definite objectives that set up the goals to be attained; it was controlled by strict rules that determined who "won" and who "lost"; and successful performance required "know-how" as well as appropriate physical prowess.

Isn't it amazing that the ancient Egyptians, Greeks, and other people of the distant past probably knew at least as many wrestling holds and stratagems as we do? Their art work indicates that they probably did. (See fig. 1.1, page 2)

Wrestling may be compared with language. That is, all peoples possess the ability and impulse to speak, but the way in which they speak depends upon where they happen to have been born. Thus, some people speak English, others French, and still others Chinese or Hopi Indian. Similarly, wrestling has taken different forms in different parts of the world. Also, as with language, some countries have produced more than one type of wrestling. The middle-Eastern and Western parts of the world evolved today's two best-known forms of wrestling—freestyle (sometimes called "catch-as-catch-can") and Greco-Roman (a combination of Greek and Roman), both of which are included in the modern Olympic Games. Interestingly, some Oriental countries that evolved "martial arts" or highly refined defensive and combative techniques such as Judo and

Who were the first people known to have strict rules to determine the winner of a wrestling match?

Fig. 1.1   "Marble Group of Pancratiasts"— Uffizi Galleries, Florence, Italy, page 253, plate 25. From Carnegie Institute of Washington Institution Publication No. 268: Olympic Victor Monuments and Greek Athletic Art. By permission.

Karate now also produce leading freestyle wrestlers who compete successfully in world competitions.

We have evolved a very satisfactory set of scholastic and collegiate wrestling rules and procedures, but they are considerably different from those used in international wrestling. However, the National Wrestling Federation and the National American Athletic Union (NAAU) have been carrying on a number of tournaments using the International Wrestling Rules. Also, world championships are being held for both junior and senior divisions. Many states are sending their state champions abroad to wrestle in international meets. At any rate, this book is about American freestyle wrestling and refers specifically to collegiate wrestling (which in turn is very similar to scholastic wrestling).

Today, wrestling is a fast growing sport in our youth organizations, schools, and colleges. Much credit for this accelerated interest is due to many coaches— such as our own coaches, E. C. Gallagher, one of America's most famous wrestling coach, who coached for years at Oklahoma A&M (now Oklahoma State University) and "Granny" Johnson, who coached for years at the University of Denver.

A final word needs to be said about American professional "rassling," which is a most strange offshoot in the historical development of wrestling. It is important to know that professional "rassling" is not "wrestling"; many

---

What two organizations in the United States have done the most to promote international wrestling in this country?

---

people criticize and reject the sport of wrestling because they think mistakenly that it is the same as the brutal display of "rassling."

Wrestling has always been a popular spectator sport. Early in this century, some wrestlers and promoters began to capitalize on this fact and to tailor-make "matches" to please the crowd. The difference between amateur wrestling and professional "rassling" can be understood quite simply in these terms. Amateur wrestling is a sport and a contest. Professional "rassling" is not. It is entertainment solely for the audience and is no more a test of skill between sportsmen than is the make-believe rough and tumble fighting in a western movie—in which the good guys also finally win out over the bad guys after being savagely thrown about and beaten!

Getting fit to wrestle

2

Competitive wrestling is one of the most strenuous of sports and requires careful conditioning. No matter how many holds and moves a person knows, he cannot hope to be even a fairly good wrestler without "wrestling fitness." Such fitness must include the entire body to an unusual degree. It is for this reason that good athletes in other sports usually cannot wrestle hard for more than one to three minutes until they have developed wrestling fitness.

Basic considerations in the development of fitness include: strength, two kinds of endurance, and power. All four need to be developed to a high degree for wrestling because of the demands that extended exertion in all kinds of positions against the vigorous resistance of an opponent place on the total body.

STRENGTH

Strength refers to how much work the muscles can perform with a single effort. Strength can be developed by means of the well-known "overload" principle, which means gradually increasing the amount that you can lift or pull with a maximum effort. For example, you lift a given maximum weight over a period of time until it becomes rather easy, then you add to the weight enough to make it difficult again, and so on. Thus, overloading means pushing yourself a little beyond what you can do easily, thereby gradually increasing what you can do. All of your muscles can be strengthened in this way.

A well-rounded program of weight training is an especially effective way of building strength. (See *Weight Training* by Philip J. Rasch, which is in this series.) Also, resistance exercises or "isometrics" are good, especially when no equipment or facilities are available. You can push against all manner of stationary objects with your body in various positions. You can lock your hands together and try to pull them apart; place your palms together and have a pushing contest between your arms; have your head resist pushing from your hands from all directions; cross your feet at the ankles and have them resist the others efforts to move; and so forth. In this way, one can get a stiff workout while sitting in a chair. If gymnastic equipment is available, the parallel and horizontal bars, the still rings, and the horse are especially good for developing upper-body strength.

BUILDING ENDURANCE

Both muscular and circulatory (heart and circulation) endurance are essential for wrestling fitness. Endurance refers to the length of time that you can continue an activity or number of repetitions Muscular endurance, that is the endurance of a particular muscle or muscle group, is developed by persisting, by repeating the strength activity. Not lifting a weight once, but over and over again is an endurance exercise. Again, the overload principle applies. If you can do fifteen pushups this week, try for seventeen—or twenty—next.

Circulatory endurance, circulation to the whole body, is developed in the same way. Continue total-body, especially leg, exertions over longer and longer periods of time. Fast walking for distance, fast rope skipping, cross country running, and running up and down hills—are all effective means of building this type of endurance. This is what will see you through a long, hard match.

POWER

Power has to do with how rapidly strength can be exerted. It is tremendously helpful to you if you can learn to explode into certain movements, such as when you go for your opponents' legs or attempt an escape. Isolate those moves where power is especially important and practice exploding your move. The good wrestler explodes just right. That is, the correct move is made, but explosively.

In addition to the foregoing, fitness for all contact sports requires a considerable degree of *toughness* that also needs to be developed. Lead-up combative games can be very helpful in acquiring rough-and-tumble toughness, and they can help to bring together the strength, endurance, and power in a wrestling-like way. Examples of such games are: (1) Attempt to push your opponent from a ten-foot circle from a standing position. Same contest from the knees. Same contest from hands and knees with head on opponent's shoulder. (2) Determine which opponent can pull the other over a line, starting not touching; start grasping hands. (3) Determine which opponent can grasp and lift the other off his feet without falling.

Of course, the chief way of getting fit for wrestling is lots of wrestling. However, the importance of the total conditioning program should not be underestimated. For example, the great Olympic champion Dan Gable had fine skills; but he submitted himself to such an intensive conditioning program of weight training, running, and calisthenics that he simply overwhelmed

---

How can you develop circulatory endurance?

---

virtually all opponents with the strength, endurance, and power with which he applied his skills.

EATING FOR FITNESS

Food intake is actually an important dimension of the total fitness program. Misconceptions about nutrition often lead athletes to overestimate certain foods and underestimate others. Modern knowledge suggests the following things about eating for wrestling (and living generally): (1) there are no magic foods that, by themselves, will give special powers—there's no substitute for hard work; (2) the best diet for the athlete (and everyone else) is one that (a) has variety, (b) is balanced—that is, it contains fruits and vegetables, grains, and proteins (from dairy products, meats, and beans), (c) and that is agreeable to the particular individual; and (3) no one food is essential in the diet, and top wrestlers have gotten along well without meat, oranges, milk, spinach, or any other of our "halo" foods. There are always substitutes of equal value that may not cost as much.

Be especially careful about eating before competitions. If you are very upset or anxious—as even some outstanding wrestlers become—food may remain undigested in your stomach. This can mean stomach upset and even cause interference with breathing during the match. High carbohydrate intake in meals prior to competition will make plenty of energy available.

MAKING WEIGHT

The best way to lose weight is to cut down on total intake while maintaining a balanced diet. This takes more planning and time than total fasting, but it is less painful, less disruptive, and less stressful to the system. Indications are that adult wrestlers can lose ten pounds without risk; but it is recommended that adolescents lose little, if any, weight because of possible ill-effects on growth.

Serious deprivation of water is dangerous (e.g., kidney damage) and should be avoided.

A NOTE OF CAUTION

We must emphasize that attempting to get into wrestling shape too quickly can lead to excessive fatigue and extreme muscular soreness—both of which can discourage the beginner from continuing. A good conditioning program, that includes dimensions of exercise, nutrition, and rest is the way to prepare the body gradually to handle the demands of the vigorous sport of wrestling.

Research insights for wrestling

3

Although relatively little scientific research has been done on wrestling as such, a considerable amount has been done on exercise and on various other sports that bear directly on wrestling. Some findings of interest follow.

EFFECTS OF TRAINING (CONDITIONING)

As physical fitness improves, the following are some of the major, beneficial changes that occur in the body: (1) strength increases; (2) coordination is improved; (3) oxygen consumption is lowered for a given amount of work; (4) there is greater capacity for maximum oxygen consumption; (5) greater heart output occurs with less increase in pulse rate and blood pressure during exercise; (6) there is greater, more efficient, lung functioning; (7) there is better utilization of oxygen in muscle and heightened ability to push oneself before exhaustion; (8) faster recovery to normal heart rate and blood pressure after exercise is found; and (9) there is better ability to get rid of body heat generated by exercise.

There is a personal limit of fitness beyond which the individual cannot go, regardless of how hard he trains. The champion must work very hard, but he must have the potential for very high-level fitness. Moreover, excessive training (i.e., too long or too frequent bouts) has been shown to give rise to chronic fatigue and "staleness." Thus, trying too hard can hurt performance.[1]

BODY BUILD OF WRESTLERS[2]

The available evidence indicates that successful wrestlers at scholastic and collegiate levels in the U.S. are not ponderous muscle men. In fact, they tend

1. See L. Brouha, "Training" and other chapters in *Science and Medicine of Exercise and Sport*, ed. W. R. Johnson and E. R. Buskirk (New York: Harper & Row, 1974).
2. See P. J. Rasch and W. Kroll, *What Research Tells the Coach about Wrestling* (Washington, D. C.: American Association for Health, Physical Education and Recreation, 1964).

7

What are some of the major beneficial changes that occur in the body as the result of a good wrestling program?

---

to be "average" and agile. At higher levels of competition, they are mostly on the muscular-lean side, although some heavyweights are not. Years of observation suggest that at lower and recreational wrestling levels, individuals with any body build can and do find enjoyment in well-conducted programs. The important thing is to match individuals so that each contestant has a fair chance.

PHYSIOLOGICAL FACTORS

Research has been done on energy cost of wrestling (about 12 times resting state), heart size of wrestlers and their electrocardiology, pulse rates, blood pressure, blood chemistry, and kidney functioning. Nothing remarkable was found among the wrestlers as compared with other athletes. There is no evidence of detrimental effects of conditioning for or participating in wrestling. In fact, as we have noted, physical conditioning improves physiological functioning.

PERSONALITY FACTORS

Although various personality tests have been administered to many athletes, including wrestlers, no pattern of traits has yet emerged as being typical of successful athletes. Research does indicate that champions and near champions are aggressive and extremely motivated to win. Many even feel that they "have to win." Of course, all of the desire in the world will get the wrestler nowhere unless it is accompanied by the necessary basic physical equipment, intensive training, skills, and quality coaching.

EMOTIONAL FACTORS

Research confirms the common observation that many if not most wrestlers, even champions, become more-or-less emotionally upset before formal matches. Symptoms may include any of the following: nervousness, "butterflies" in the stomach, fear (even though there is little likelihood of getting hurt), inability to sleep well or even at all a night or more before the match and/or a night after, tiredness, inability to concentrate, grouchiness, and so on.

Emotion often involves the body readying itself for action; and various distractions ranging from movies to dancing may serve to keep body adjustments in check. However, emotional upset is often based on worry: worry over losing, looking bad, failing the team, and what not. In brief, the wrestler agonizes over what might happen. Distractions may provide such wrestlers little relief. Howev-

What does research show about the energy cost of wrestling?

er, research in psychotherapy has helpful suggestions to offer. One technique is to have the individual imagine vividly the very worst thing that can happen in the match. Now what would the actual consequences of that be? Really all that terrible? Will you be taken out and shot? Rejected by society? Of course not! Great relief can follow such a simple approach.

Equipment, safety, sanitation, and injuries

4

Considerable attention should be given to equipment, safety, and sanitation. Your enjoyment of the sport will be increased and you will incur fewer injuries if you do so. Knowledge of the rules is a requirement, of course, for participation; strict adherence to them also assures safe conditions.

EQUIPMENT

Personal   The personal equipment for a wrestler should consist of wrestling shoes, sweat socks, tights and shorts, supporter, athletic shirt, and wrestling helmet. The equipment, of course, should always be kept clean.

Wrestling Mats   The mat should be made of ensolite material about an inch in thickness. It should be about 35 feet-by-35 feet with a circle 28 feet in diameter. There should be a 10-foot circle in the center of the mat.

Safety and Sanitation   Generally speaking, wrestling is not a dangerous sport because practically all of the dangerous holds have been removed. Here are some safety and sanitation precautions, however, that are the responsibility of all who participate in wrestling:

1. Do not participate in wrestling without a physician's permission.
2. Be sure to warm up properly.
3. Condition yourself gradually to wrestling.
4. Do not use questionable holds.
5. Never try to hurt an opponent.
6. Keep fingernails trimmed.
7. Do not wear rings or other jewelery.
8. Do not wrestle close to walls, standards, or other objects.
9. Do not wrestle in an overcrowed area.

What are some of the most common errors made in the use of personal equipment?

10. Wear proper equipment.
11. Do not wrestle if you have any infection.
12. Do not lounge around after a hard match. Keep moving.
13. Do not cool off too quickly. Put on a sweat suit or take a shower.
14. Keep all personal equipment clean.
15. Be sure mats are clean and disinfected.

Wrestling Injuries   There are a few injuries that occur most often in wrestling and others that are common in all sports.

Cauliflower ears—caused by the rubbing of ears together. Wear helmet and there will be no problem.

Impetigo, boils, ringworm, and athlete's foot—caused by unsanitary personal equipment or unsanitary mats or by working with someone who has these infections.

Broken bones, dislocations, and pulled cartilages—caused generally by illegal holds or potentially dangerous holds.

Sprains—caused by improper falling to mats or by forcing the joint beyond normal movement.

Basic takedowns

5

The techniques that comprise the basic fundamental skills of wrestling are presented in this book. A mastery of these skills should be the goal of every beginner, since they will enable him to progress more rapidly. It is important that the wrestler have proper instruction and then make the correct application when trying to master these fundamentals. Since there is no one way to wrestle and because no two wrestlers are built exactly the same, each wrestler should be permitted to develop his own style.

ILLUSTRATIONS

In these illustrations, the moves described are demonstrated by the wrestler with the dark uniform. He is always referred to as wrestler "A." All holds described are shown in the illustrations from one side only. Any move or hold can be executed from either side, however, and should be so practiced.

WRESTLING ON YOUR FEET

The champions of today are very clever on their feet and are excellent takedown artists. Some of the greatest thrills and cleverest moves in wrestling are the results of takedowns. The takedowns that are used must be adapted to fit individual build, speed, and agility. The stance one uses is very important in determining how effective he will be in defending himself and attacking his opponent.

Consider these factors when determining the stance you will use.

1. Can you defend yourself against the most common takedowns, maneuvers, and counters?

2. Do you have maneuverability from this position?

Why is it so important to master the basic skills of wrestling in good form?

---

3. Are you comfortable and relaxed?
4. Can you attack and explode from this position?
5. Do you have good balance?

There are two basic stances used today. These are the square stance and the staggered stance. The square stance allows better lateral movement, and in this stance one can attack from either leg. The staggered stance allows you to attack straight forward; it is quicker and you can penetrate deeper. However, you don't have quite as much lateral movement.

Footwork—Good footwork is essential to all sports, but it is so fundamental to the wrestler maintaining his balance that certain basic admonitions are listed below as coaching points and common mistakes. Correct footwork must be practiced until it becomes automatic.

Coaching points:

1. Move quickly on the balls of the feet.
2. Take short steps and slide the feet on the mat.
3. Keep relaxed so you can move quickly.
4. Keep your feet moving.
5. Keep your shoulder and knee perpendicular to one another in order to maintain good balance.
6. Keep elbows in close to the sides of the body.

Common mistakes:

1. Reaching for your opponent when too far out.
2. Taking long steps.
3. Crossing feet when moving.
4. Approaching your opponent with elbows out and away from body.
5. Pressing your opponent or leaning on him.
6. Failing to keep moving.

Most tie-up positions:

1. Neck and elbow—A grasps his opponent's neck with his right hand (note palm of hand is on top of neck) and holds B's right elbow with his left hand with thumb up. A's head is against B's right shoulder. Wrestler B will have the same position on A. This is not a good offensive position.
2. Open position—In this position neither wrestler has contact with his opponent. Each wrestler is looking for an opening in his opponent's defense.
3. Neck bicep position—A grasps his opponent's neck with his right hand and grasps B at the biceps just above the elbow with his left hand (fingers on top, thumb down). This is an excellent offensive position.

4. Double biceps position—A grasps B's both biceps with his hands from the inside of B's elbow; however, B can change to A's position very quickly. Here again, both wrestlers are in excellent offensive positions.
5. Neck and over-arm positions—A grasps his opponent's neck with his right hand. A then comes over B's right arm with his left arm. He grasps B's right arm just above the right elbow with his left hand with thumb up. A should make B carry his weight (excellent position for fireman carry).
6. Inside and outside grip—A has gripped B's left wrist with his right hand from the inside. At the same time he grasps B's right wrist with his left hand from outside. (This shows the different positions of controlling the wrist. They both have their advantages and disadvantages.)
7. The outside upper-arm and wrist position—As B comes into A, A grasps B's left wrist with his left hand. Then A slides to the outside of B's left arm, grasps B's left arm above the elbow with his right hand. A now has control of B's upper arm and wrist.

DOUBLE LEG TACKLE

1. Wrestler A assumes the neck, biceps tie-up position, however, it can be worked from almost any position.
2. A ducks his head quickly and jerks B's head and arms forward. A steps deep with his right foot.
3. A lands on his right knee followed with left knee to mat. Keep both knees moving. The head should be on the outside of your opponent's hip.
4. A brings his left leg forward and to the outside. He snaps his head back and into B's side and starts pivoting on his right knee. He has a loose grip on B's legs.
5. A pivots around and moves his arm around B's wrist and straddles B's right legs.

Coaching points:

1. Must have a good set-up by getting past your opponent's arms.
2. Must penetrate deep into opponent's legs.
3. Keep shoulders and knee perpendicular to the mat for good balance.
4. Head must go on the outside of the hips.
5. Must have good contact with head and shoulders.
6. Keep knees moving.
7. Always take opponent to the mat with head on top.
8. Always explode on your opponent.

Most common mistakes:

1. Going for legs when too far out.
2. Poor set-up.

Why is deep penetration so important on a double leg tackle, and why should your shoulder and knee be kept perpendicular to the mat?

Neck and Elbow

Open Position

Neck Bicep Position

Double Biceps

Neck and Over Arm Position

Inside and Outside Grip

The Outside Upper and Wrist Position

Fig. 5.1   Most Common Tie-up Positions

Fig. 5.2   Double Leg Tackle

3. Not exploding on your opponent.
4. Elbows too far out and away from the body.
5. Reaching for the head from too far out.
6. Poor penetration, by not stepping deep enough into your opponent.
7. Not hitting the mat with the front inside knee first.
8. Over extending the body, which put you in a poor position.
9. Taking your opponent to the mat with your head underneath.

SINGLE LEG TACKLE

1. The set-up here is a little different than the double leg in that you are concentrating on securing one leg.
2. A circles to his right forcing B to take longer steps with his right leg. A shoves B's right arm up. Take a deep step to the outside of B's right leg. At the same time A drops on his right knee right in front of B's right foot.
3. A places his head on the inside of B's right thigh. At the same time he hooks his left arm around back of B's knee. His right hand grasps B's right ankle.
4. A rotates his knees by pulling his right knee up off of the mat. At the same time he places his left knee on the mat back and between B's legs.

5. A pulls B's right foot off the mat and snaps B's right knee forward to the mat for a take down.

Coaching points:

1. The set-up involves getting B to take longer strides with the leg you want.
2. The penetration must be deep and to the outside.
3. Head must be to the inside of the thigh.
4. The top arm should be around the outside and back of the knee.
5. The bottom hand should be on the inside of the ankle.
6. The knees should be rotated cutting your opponent forward.
7. You must have balance and control of your opponent.
8. Don't go to the mat unless your opponent is down on the mat.

Fig. 5.3   Single Leg Tackle

Common mistakes:

1. Not making your opponent move into you.
2. Deep penetration with outside leg.
3. Not putting the head on the inside of the thigh.
4. Not keeping shoulder and knee perpendicular to the mat.
5. Not rotating the knees or snapping the opponent forward.
6. Getting on both knees at the same time.

7. If you pick your opponent's leg up never go to the mat until your opponent is down.

FIREMAN CARRY

1. Wrestler A assumes the neck, biceps tie-up position, keeping the head low.
2. A ducks under B's arm quickly, holding the arm tightly around neck. At the same time A drops to his left knee with his right leg between B's legs.
3. A places the right arm up B's crotch. A snaps down B's right arm and picks B up with right arm in B's crotch. At the same time A is driving off his right foot.
4. A throws B on his right shoulder and takes him down with his back to the mat.
5. A pulls his arm out of B's crotch and places it around B's waist, driving him on to the mat in a pinning situation.

Coaching points:

1. Must take a deep step with inside foot in order to penetrate deep.
2. Arm must be securely tight around neck.
3. Must drop on one knee with other leg between opponent's legs. This gives power to the move.
4. Must be sure to stand the opponent's shoulder to mat.

Fig. 5.4 Fireman Carry

5. Must bend knees to get under.
6. Must make a good set-up.

Common mistakes:

1. Dropping on both knees (no power).
2. Failing to put leg between legs to get power.
3. Failing to keep arm tight around neck.
4. Failing to get hand up crotch. (Not as good control.)
5. Failing to penetrate deep.
6. Failing to take advantage of pinning situation.

DUCK UNDER

1. A grasps B's neck with his right hand. As he reaches for B's neck, A slides his left hand to the inside of B's right arm and grasps the bicep.
2. A puts pressure on B's right arm by pulling down in order to arm drag him. As B resists this pressure by pulling his arm up, A ducks under B's right arm.
3. A then snaps back up on B's right arm with his head, at the same time using his right hand to pull down on B's neck.
4. A swings wide, snapping down on B's neck and at the same time grasps B's back crotch with his left hand, thus driving B forward and down to the mat.

Coaching points:

1. When ducking under arm be sure to bend your knee. It will make your move much quicker.
2. Step forward with your outside leg to penetrate deep.
3. Once under arm snap head up and back by straightening your knees.
4. Snap down on opponent's neck.

Fig. 5.5 Duck Under

5. Use the hand in back crotch to force him to the mat.
6. Do a good set-up on arm ducking under. Put pressure down on arm as if to drag.

Common mistakes:

1. Not bending knees to get under arm.
2. Not putting pressure down on arm to get opponent to resist up.
3. Not exploding.
4. Failing to penetrate deep.
5. Failing to snap head back and up.
6. Not snapping down on neck swinging wide.
7. Failing to put a lot of force in back crotch.

ARM DRAG

1. Wrestler A ties-up in a neck and bicep position, when B starts to push A.
2. A jerks B's right arm to A's right, putting most of his power in right arm pit and using his left hand to guide B's right elbow past A.
3. At the same time A moves past B's right side and hooks his right leg around B's right ankle, leasing B's right elbow. A then reaches behind B's right leg with his left hand and swings B to the mat.
4. A pulls down and forward with his right hand and swings his buttocks out and comes on top with his leg over B's right leg.

Coaching points:

1. In this type of arm drag B must be pushing A resisting a duck under.
2. Must get your opponent's arm past your body.
3. Must snap forward and down on the arm.

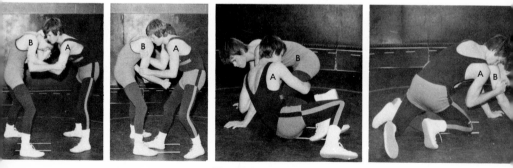

Fig. 5.6   Arm Drag

4. Swing buttocks out and keep the outside leg outside of B's leg.
5. Pull down on B's arm and at same time pull B's leg forward.

Common mistakes:

1. Not setting your opponent up.
2. Not getting arm past body.
3. Not pulling forward and down on arm.
4. Not swinging the buttocks out.
5. Not using the arm behind the thigh.

NECK AND CROSS HEEL PICK-UP

1. A grasps B's neck with his right hand and at the same time he grasps B's left arm just above the elbow. A moves to B's right pulling down on B's neck forcing B to bring his left foot forward.
2. Then A moves back to his right, dropping to his right knee near B's left foot, at the same time grasping B's left heel. He pulls B's left heel to B's right at the same time pulling B's neck down to the right.
3. B will come to the mat in the position as shown.

Coaching points:

1. Must keep B's head down.
2. Must force B to take a longer step with his left foot.
3. Must grasp the bottom of the heel for added leverage.
4. Must snap neck to your right and heel to your left.

Fig. 5.7   Neck and Cross Heel

Common mistakes:

1. Not getting head down.
2. Not forcing B's left foot well forward.

3. Not dropping on your knee close to B's foot.
4. Failing to get a quick snap on heel and neck.

NECK AND HEEL

1. A grasps B's neck with his right hand as he grasps B's left arm just above the elbow. A moves to his right, pulling down on B's neck, forcing B to bring his right foot forward.
2. A drops down on his left knee toward B's right foot and grasps B's right heel. A then pushes B's head to his left and pulls B's right heel to his right.
3. B will fall in the position shown in Illustration 3.

Coaching points:

1. Must pressure B's neck down.
2. Must pull B's right foot toward you.
3. Grasp B's heel when weight is on that foot.
4. When snapping neck keep your elbow down and in.

Common mistakes:

1. Not pulling head down.
2. Not forcing B to bring his right foot well forward.
3. Not snapping the head with elbow down and in.
4. Failing to step deep toward B's right foot.

Fig. 5.8 Neck and Heel

ELBOW AND HEEL

1. A grasps B's right elbow with his left hand as he grasps B's left bicep. A moves to his left, pulling B's bicep toward him, forcing B to bring his left foot toward him.
2. A drops down on his right knee at B's foot and at the same time he grasps

B's left heel. A then snaps B's elbow to his right, and pulls B's heel to his left.

3. B will fall in the position shown in fig. 5.9 on page 23.

Coaching points:

1. Must get B's left foot planted well forward.
2. As A goes for heel he must snap elbow through.
3. Also A must snap his head to his right.
4. B's weight must be on his left foot.

Common mistakes:

1. Not getting B's left foot well forward.
2. Not getting B's weight on his left foot.
3. A not snapping his head through hard.
4. Not snapping opponent's elbow through as he reaches for heel.

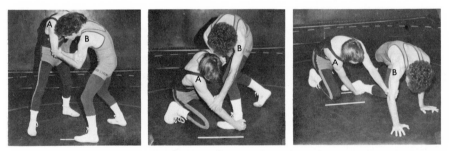

Fig. 5.9   Elbow and Heel

UNDER HOOK AND HEEL

1. A tie-up with B with an under hook and biceps position. A moves to his left pulling down on B's right shoulder with the under hook and pulling by the biceps toward you.
2. As A goes for B's left heel he shoves B to his left forcing B to put all his weight on B's left foot. A pulls up on B's left heel and B will go to the mat as shown in fig. 5.10 on page 24.

Coaching points:

1. The set-up is the key to success.
2. Must pull B into a circle and force long step with B's left foot.
3. Must shove through B's right shoulder forcing all the weight on his left foot.
4. Snap his left heel toward you.

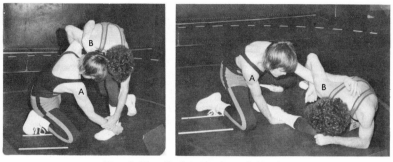

Fig. 5.10 Under Hook and Heel

Common mistakes:

1. Not pulling down on B's shoulder.
2. Not grasping B's heel before you shove through on B's shoulder.
3. Not making B take a long stride with his left foot.

Counters for takedowns

6

Countermoves are an essential part of wrestling. When one learns how to make an offensive attack on his feet, he should also soon learn how to counter that attack because every wrestling hold can be countered. A beginner when he wrestles with a more experienced person, may become discouraged because his opponent can counter every move he makes. But he will soon learn that by using some diversionary moves or fakes he can set his opponent up in spite of his efforts to counter.

Sometimes a wrestler is referred to as a "counter wrestler." This means he prefers to wait until his opponent initiates an offensive maneuver. Then he counters. This type of wrestler is one who tries to take advantage of his opponent's mistakes.

A good rule to follow is to learn the offensive moves first. After one is able to execute them with a fair degree of proficiency, he should then learn the counters.

The most common method of countering takedowns will be illustrated.

COUNTER TO DOUBLE LEG TACKLE

Hip lock counter:

1. As soon as his opponent has penetrated deep under him, A sprawls out on him. Keeping legs straight and spread out, making B carry all his weight, A reaches back with his right arm and places it under B's left armpit and grasps the back of his own right leg.
2. A pulls B forward with the right arm by snapping his own right leg straight and free of B's left arm. Note legs are well spread to give good balance.
3. A then swings to his left and comes even with B in a neutral position.

Can you define the term counter wrestler?

Coaching points:

1. Sprawl must be made quickly.
2. Give ground when opponent keeps charging.
3. Knees must not be on the mat. Keep legs straight.
4. Develop a hard snap with right hip and arm cutting B forward.
5. Once the under person grip on leg is broken snap legs straight and come even.

Common mistakes:

1. Having knees on mat.
2. Moving legs to left in the maneuver.
3. Not snapping legs straight.
4. Not hitting your opponent with hip lock more than once.
5. Not giving ground with opponent.

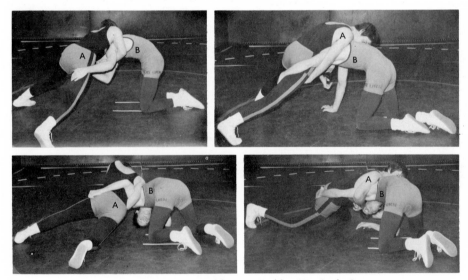

Fig. 6.1 Counter to Double Leg Tackle: Hip Lock Counter

COUNTER TO SINGLE LEG TACKLE

Hip lock counter:

1. As soon as his opponent drops under him, A flattens on him. Keeping both legs straight and spread out, making B carry all his weight, A reaches back with his right arm and places it under B's left armpit and grasps the back of his own right leg.

2.   A cuts B forward with his right arm by snapping his own right leg straight and free of B's grip on A's leg.

3.   A is then free to move for a go behind or for an escape.

Coaching points:

1.   Snap leg back and straight as you sprawl on B.

2.   As you cut B with a hip lock be sure to snap your right leg straight and hard.

3.   Quick reaction is a must for this move.

Common mistakes:

1.   Knees on the mat.

2.   Trying to move your feet.

3.   Not hitting your opponent hard with hip lock more than once.

4.   Not giving ground with your opponent.

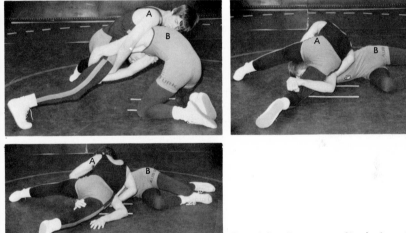

Fig. 6.2   Counter to Single Leg: Hip Lock Counter

COUNTER TO ARM DRAG

Counter drag:

1.   As B brings A to the mat with an arm drag, A grasps B's left arm near the armpit.

2.   A jerks B's right arm to A's right, putting most of his power in right armpit and using his left hand to guide B's right elbow past A.

3.   A sits through by pivoting on his left foot, snaps B's left arm forward with his own left hand.

4.   A snaps forward on B's left arm and swings out to his right. A grasps B's back crotch with his right hand and swings wide to come on top.

Coaching points:

1. A must make his move when B is bringing him to the mat. Timing is very important.
2. Pivot under your opponent hard and snap him forward.
3. Get a good grip on a back crotch pulling forward.
4. Control opponents legs by your legs and hands.

Common mistakes:

1. Poor timing.
2. Not using your opponent's momentum.
3. Failing to put a lot of pressure forward in your opponent's crotch.

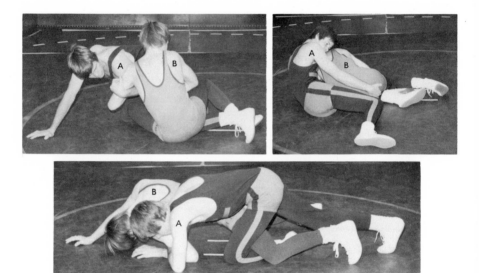

Fig. 6.3   Counter to Arm Drag: Counter Drag

COUNTER TO DUCK UNDER

Near wing and cross over:

1. As they come to the mat by a duck under, A hooks B's upper arm and snaps down. At the same time he shifts his weight to his right foot. A throws his left leg up and over B as he has B's arm under him.
2. A crosses completely over B which brings him under control.

Coaching points:

1. Timing is very important.

2. The snap down on the arm must be hard to knock your opponent off his base.
3. The inside foot must be lifted high over opponent.

Common mistakes:

1. Not getting a good grip on the opponent's arm for a wing.
2. Not hitting when off balance.
3. Not throwing inside leg high above opponent.

Fig. 6.4   Counter to Duck Under: Near Wing and Cross-over

COUNTER TO FIREMAN CARRY

Shuck:

1. As B goes for a fireman carry, A flattens out on B and thrusts his right arm into B's thigh. He must be careful to keep parallel with B.
2. A then grasps B's left arm just above the elbow with his right hand. At the same time he grasps B's at the arm pit.
3. A then grasps B's left ankle with his right hand. A tries to move behind B by going to his right, and B tries to prevent this by moving away from A.
4. As A gets B moving to his left, A thrusts B's head to his left. At the same time A moves back to his left.
5. A then moves behind B for the counters.

Coaching points:

1. A must get B moving his legs away from A or A can cradle B.
2. Once A gets motion out of B he can snap B to his right.
3. Be quick to change direction.

Common mistakes:

1. Failing to stop B's thrust for legs.
2. Failing to sprawl, leg spread.
3. Not getting the movement out of B.

Fig. 6.5   Counter to Fireman Carry: Shuck

Takedowns from behind

7

There are two distinct situations that may develop during the course of a wrestling match in which a wrestler may find himself behind his opponent in a standing position. The first occurs when he gets behind while he and his adversary are both on their feet. The second occurs when he has control on the mat and his opponent jumps to his feet while underneath.

When A is behind his opponent in standing position, he keeps his feet about a foot behind and parallel to B's feet. A keeps his arms locked tightly around B's waist and his hands locked tightly together on one hip. This makes it harder for B to break A's grip and at the same time gives A more leverage. The double arm bar can be used very effectively on B also.

If B leans forward, or tries to move away from A, the outside leg trip or waist lock pick-up can be used very effectively. If he stands up straight or pushes back into A, A can use a back heel with knee in crotch or a waist lock pick-up to his advantage. Speed and deception are a decisive factor in these maneuvers.

OUTSIDE LEG TRIP

1. A is behind his opponent with his feet parallel with B.
2. A hooks his left leg over B's left leg, shoving him forward with all his weight.
3. A uses his right arm around B's waist cutting to his left hard. Just before he hits the mat A disengages his right arm so B cannot counter. A has B's left foot hooked by his right leg. He now moves up on B.

Coaching points:

1. B must be moving forward or leaning.

Under what circumstances may a wrestler find himself standing behind his opponent?

Fig. 7.1   Outside Leg Trip

2. As A has B moving toward the mat he must cut B to his left hard.
3. Arm must not be around waist when B hits the mat or B can counter.

WAIST LOCK PICK-UP WITH KNEE TAP:

1. A has a waist lock around B's waist. He snaps his hips into B's buttock, forcing B's legs off the mat.
2. A then taps B's with his left knee causing B to tilt to his left.
3. This puts B's legs out of position to catch his balance and takes B onto the mat.

Coaching points:

1. Grip tightly around waist.
2. Snap hip hard in his opponent's buttock.

Fig. 7.2   Waist Lock Pick-up with Knee Tap

3. Knee tap his opponent's knee to throw B off balance.
4. Drop to knees immediately with opponent.

BACK HEEL WITH KNEE IN CROTCH

1. A puts his left foot on B's left heel with a waist lock around B's waist. A keeps his left leg straight and as he goes to the mat with B he throws his right knee into B's back crotch.
2. A falls on his left hip as he hits the mat with B.
3. A keeps knee in B's back crotch.

Coaching points:

1. Your opponent must not be leaning or moving forward.
2. The heel leg must be straight.
3. Knee must be kept in your opponent's back crotch. This prevents counters.

Fig. 7.3   Back Heel with Knee in Crotch

Breakdowns and rides

8

One of the most important aspects of wrestling is breaking the opponent down and keeping him under control. The reason coaches place so much emphasis on this phase of the sport is that it is preliminary to securing a fall. If a wrestler cannot control his opponent, the possibility of pinning him becomes very remote, and if he tries to pin him without bringing him under control he puts himself in a very dangerous situation. It turns out to be a rough and tumble affair in which either man can get pinned. The wrestler's first objective after bringing his opponent to the mat is to flatten him out in a prone position. By getting B in this position, A has accomplished a threefold objective: first, he has eliminated the possibility of B's escape by destroying his base; second, A has put B in a position where he can be pinned; and third, A has gained a chance to relax after shooting hard.

Breakdowns   A breakdown is the flattening of an opponent down on the mat in a prone position. When A is on top, he must recognize that the underneath man, B, has four points of support very similar to a table. The object is to destroy one of these supports. B is well supported when A shoves him straight forward, backward, or to the side. The best way to destroy one of these points of the base is to drive B at a 45-degree angle. This puts him at a disadvantage because he cannot call on his other points of support to aid him. Therein lies his weakness.

Rides   Riding is the act of maintaining control of an opponent after he is flattened out on the mat. After B is broken down, A keeps his weight well distributed, making B carry it. At the same time, A maintains his own balance. This is the best way to wear B down, but A must not make the mistake of using his strength to hold B down. Instead, he should use all the weight and leverage he can in order to control and tire B. B may lose his poise, become frantic, and throw himself open, thus giving A a chance to pin him. (A coach, incidentally, cannot teach a wrestler much about either poise or

---

What is a prone position in wrestling, and what are three reasons for wanting your opponent in this position?

---

balance. The qualities are self-taught and self-developed and achieved only after long hours of hard practice.)

Starting Position:

It is always better to study the rule book on the starting position, particularly the top position, as this has changed so often. Here are a few guidelines for the bottom position that have not changed over the years:
1. You must establish a solid base for the underneath position.
2. Keep a low center of gravity.
3. Keep a wide base.
4. The arms must be kept out in front with your weight on them.
5. Use the mat for resistance when opponent pulls on your arms.
6. Keep head up.

Fig. 8.1 Starting Position

HEAD LEVER AND TIGHT WAIST

1. A slides his left hand down to B's left wrist as he places his head in B's left armpit.
2. He drives his head forward, pulling B's left arm backward and to the side. At the same time he uses his right arm around B's waist to pull him onto his shoulder at a 45-degree angle.
3. As soon as A gets B's left shoulder to the mat, using his head as a lever, he takes a tighter grip on B's waist with his right arm. His shoulder should be in B's rib cage.

Coaching points:
1. Don't pull the arm straight back, but out to the side and then back.
2. Once the arm is off the mat pull the defensive man to your left breaking him down on his side.

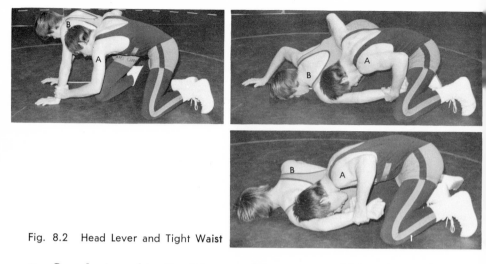

Fig. 8.2 Head Lever and Tight Waist

3. Once he is on his side slide your right arm around his waist until your elbow touches the mat. Bring the right knee up against his hip; then pull him against the knee. Keep B's left arm off the mat.

HEAD LEVER AND DOUBLE BAR

1. Once B is broken down as in number three in the Head Lever and Tight Wrist, A slides B's left arm under B and grasps both hands around B's

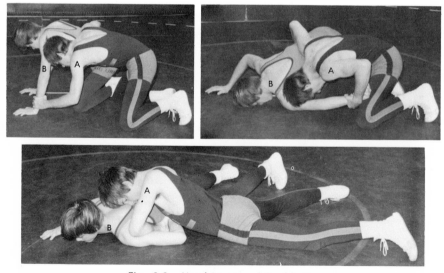

Fig. 8.3 Head Lever and Double Bar

left wrist. A shoves his left elbow forward and puts pressure on the upper part of B's left arm. At the same time he pries up on B's right wrist.

Coaching points:

1. Be sure you put all the weight you can on B's shoulder.
2. If he gets up on his knees bring your left knee and place it against the elbow so he can't get his arm out.
3. Then you are free to use your right hand to grasp his far ankle or get a back crotch. This keeps your opponent under control.

FAR ANKLE AND NEAR WAIST

1. From a referee position on top, A reaches across with his right hand and grasps his opponent's right instep. He places his left arm around B's waist. From this position he breaks B down in a prone position.

Coaching points:

1. Always grasp the instep for more leverage on the foot.
2. Once you have him in a prone position on the mat tighten up his far arm.

GROIN RIDE

1. Break your opponent as under far ankle and near waist.
2. Then A forces B's right foot forward and brings his own right leg over and around the opponents right foot. B's right ankle will be resting in A's groin. A keeps pressure on the right instep as he ties his opponent's right arm in a double bar.

Coaching points:

1. Once you get B's right foot in your groin, be sure you keep your right knee in advance position on B's foot.
2. When B tries to get out of this position he will leave himself in position to get pinned.

Fig. 8.4   Far Ankle and Near Waist

Fig. 8.5   Groin Ride

OVER AND UNDER RIDE

1. From a referee position on top, A reaches across with his right han grasps his opponent's right instep. A places his left arm around B's A snaps B's right leg back across his knee and locks his arm arour right leg.
2. A places his left hand behind B's right ankle. A moves back. Wi right arm around B's waist, he pulls B toward him as he forces B's ankle up.
3. Then A drops into B's crotch with his left elbow to the mat. He his right arm around B's waist. If B raises up on his right elbow, A it out from under him, using his right hand. A must keep his weigh back.

Fig. 8.6   Over and Under Ride

Coaching points:

1. The leg must be snatched back hard and to you; at the same time, pull your opponent toward you.
2. You must grasp his right ankle for leverage. This is very important.
3. Your left elbow must be kept in contact with the mat.
4. Shift weight back and flatten out. This takes away your opponent's leverage and gives you more leverage.

FAR ANKLE AND FAR ARM

1. A reaches across with his left hand and grasps his opponent's left instep. With the right hand he reaches across and grasps the opponent's left arm just above the elbow.
2. A pulls B's left arm toward him and forces B's left instep forward. He then forces B to the mat on his left shoulder.

Coaching points:

1. Be sure you grasp B at his instep to get better leverage.
2. Be sure you grasp B's right elbow at the elbow in order to get better leverage.

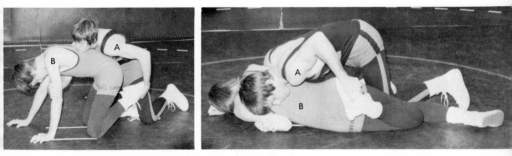

Fig. 8.7   Far Ankle Far Arm

Counters for breakdowns and rides

9

It is imperative that a wrestler know all the basic counters to arm and leg breakdowns. He must be able to maintain a good base to operate from and never allow his opponent an opportunity to get good leverage on his position. The best defense is to take the offense immediately.

When his arms and legs are tied up, he must know how to free them. Then he must take the offense quickly, forcing his opponent on the defense.

COUNTER FOR THE HEAD LEVER

Arm Roll:

1. As B uses his head lever to pry A's left arm back, A resists with everything he has. This will set B up for the arm roll.
2. Then all of a sudden, A turns his left wrist in with the palm of the hand up as shown in the illustration. He drops his left elbow to the mat and frees his arm.

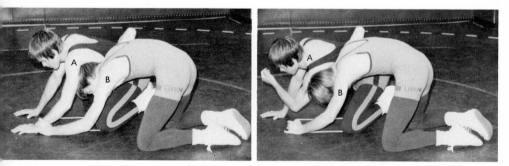

Fig. 9.1   Counter for Head Lever: Arm Roll

Why are the simple counters so important in maintaining a good base?
Why are they important for starting offensive maneuvers?

Coaching points:

1. Set-up B by resisting pressure.
2. Then explode by rolling your wrist up.

COUNTER FOR THE HEAD LEVER

Wrist Twist:

1. As B uses head lever to pry A's left arm back, A resists with everything he has. This will set B up for the wrist twist.
2. Then all of a sudden, A goes with B's pressure turning his left wrist and hand up and over B's left wrist.
3. This twists his wrist out of B's grip, freeing his arm.

Coaching points:

1. After resisting B's pressure explode with your left hand up and over B's wrist.
2. This is the time to explode on a move to reverse or escape.

Fig. 9.2   Counter for Head Lever: Wrist Twist

COUNTER FOR SINGLE BAR ARM

Elbow Twist:

1. Wrestler B has A's left wrist tied up in a single bar arm with B's left hand.
2. A straightens his left arm out as shown.
3. He then turns his elbow back into B's elbow, then turns his forearm up, and his arm is free.

Coaching points:

1. Once arm is straight, throw elbow back into opponent's elbow.
2. This gives A leverage on B's hand and breaks the grip.

Fig. 9.3   Counter for Single Bar: Elbow Twist

COUNTER FOR DOUBLE BAR ARM

Under and Over:

1. A puts his right arm under B's right forearm and grasps B's left wrist with his right hand.

Fig. 9.4   Counter for Double Bar: Under and Over

2. A then pries up on B's right forearm, shoving down on B's left wrist with his right hand. At the same time, A turns his left wrist down and pries up with left forearm. The timing is important.
3. A then throws his left elbow back into B's elbow and comes free.

Coaching points:

1. A must work both arms at the same time.
2. Snap both arms straight down.

COUNTER FOR FAR ARM

Shoulder Drop:

1. B reaches across under A to grasp his right arm just above the elbow for a breakdown.
2. A drops his shoulders and bends his elbows out so B cannot reach A's right arm.

Fig. 9.5   Counter for Far Arm: Shoulder Drop

COUNTER FOR OVER AND UNDER RIDE

Bridge Up and Turn Away:

1. B has an over and under ride on A. A assumes a position for his counter attack by placing his left elbow in position as shown in fig. 9.6, bringing his legs up in position to raise his buttock off the mat.
2. A lifts his buttock high off the mat to get in good position to use leverage for the turn. A throws his left leg over his right leg in a scissor motion on B's left arm. This breaks B's ride.

Coaching points:

1. Snap buttocks quickly up and turn with a hard snap.
2. B must pull his arm out or go with your move.

Fig. 9.6 Counter for Over and Under Ride: Bridge Lip and Turn Away

Reverses and escapes

10

Escaping from underneath position to the feet (one point), or better still, reversing from underneath to top position (two points) are important wrestling techniques to learn. It requires a keen sense of balance, deception, and timing to work out maneuvers from the underneath position. Keep in mind the location of the opponent's legs and arms and learn to recognize immediately what reverses or escapes could be used most effectively in this position.

The wrestler must always stay in position by never allowing his arms and legs to get "tied up." If he does get tied up, he will be in trouble unless he immediately fights free.

If a contestant uses escape variations, it is important that he be especially good on takedowns. Once he escapes and is behind in points, he must secure a takedown to regain lost ground. If he reverses, however, he doesn't lose points and stands a good chance of gaining points by controlling his opponent. When a reverse is secured, it often leaves the adversary in a bad situation, one that may result in a fall or a near fall. A wrestler who uses the reverse has a distinct advantage.

Switch:

1. A brings his left arm across to his right so his opponent cannot counter by catching his left arm.
2. A shifts all his weight to his left hand and right foot as he raises his right knee off the mat.
3. A pivots on his right foot and brings his left leg through to his right. At the same time he throws his right arm over B's right arm and puts it in B's crotch, swinging wide to put pressure on B's right shoulder.

What does a wrestler score when he reverses from underneath and comes on top of his opponent?

In order to score escapes and reverses what must you do to be able to keep free?

---

4. A swings his buttock away from B to get more leverage and takes his left hand and reaches for a rear crotch.
5. He pulls B forward and comes on top.

Coaching points:

1. A must throw his left arm far enough away so B cannot catch it.
2. Don't move your right foot, just pivot on it.
3. Never sit on your buttock when you pivot out. Swing to your inside hip or this maneuver is a failure.
4. Never put your arm around your opponent's waist when you come on top since this gives your opponent a switch. Always grab a back crotch.

Fig. 10.1 Switch

Short Set Out:

1. A grasps B's right hand with his right hand.
2. At the same time he flips his feet to his right and sets over his legs so B cannot grab his foot.

3. He backs over his legs keeping his shoulders out in front of his hips.
4. As B backs off from him he then scoots out from under B, putting pressure on B's right shoulder. He holds B's right arm tight around his waist.
5. As he scoots out, he turns in on his left shoulder and pivots on left knee and shoulder; he is now facing B.

Coaching points:

1. This is the best of the set out maneuvers. You can tie this in with the Granby.
2. You must keep your left hand pressuring the mat and more to the front so you can use the mat for resistance.
3. You must keep control of his right hand so he cannot cradle you.
4. You must keep your shoulders in front of your hips so he cannot snap you back.
5. Be sure you drop on your inside shoulder and not on your elbow. He will break your arm down.
6. You may turn either way but fake him.

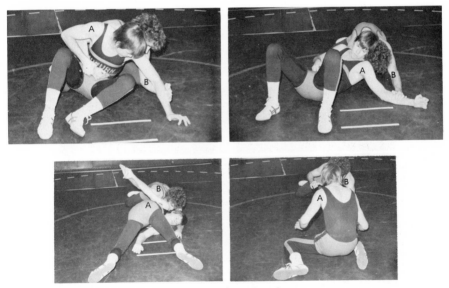

Fig. 10.2   Short Set Out

Wing Lock:

1. A grasps B's right wrist with his right hand and sets his legs up under B with A's left leg up against B's stomach and his left foot outside of B's right hip. At the same time A drops on his right hip and right elbow.

2. A is now ready to lift B up with his thigh and kick him over on his side.
3. A throws his legs perpendicular to B's body so that B is unable to roll him. A has a tight grip on B's right wrist.
4. A then shifts his weight on his right foot and then kicks his left leg through to his left. A is in a good pinning situation.

Coaching points:

1. A must get B on top of him by sitting up under him.
2. Be sure you drop on elbow; if you don't, you will get yourself in a pinning situation.
3. Once you turn him over pivot on your right foot and kick your left leg under to get perpendicular.
4. Hold his arm tight around you to get into a pinning situation.

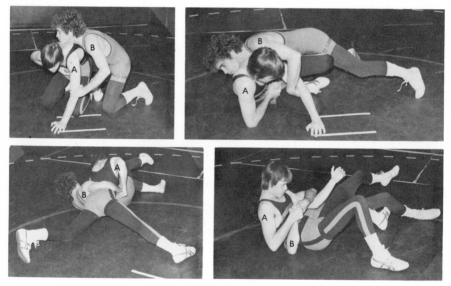

Fig. 10.3   Wing Lock

Hip Lock:

1. A hooks his left arm over B's right arm, and at the same time he raises his inside knee off the mat and pivots his right foot to the right.
2. He then whips B in circle motion, cutting him forward and downward to the right.
3. At the same time he rotates his left knee to the mat and his right knee comes off the mat.

4. A kicks his left leg up and snaps it free from B's leg. He immediately pivots and faces B.

Coaching points:

1. A must swing his left arm forward and up and over B's right arm.
2. A must snap his inside hip away from B by raising his inside knee.
3. To maintain his balance he must swing his right foot out. This gives him a good base.
4. He must try to put B's head in the mat where A has his right hand.
5. The rotary motion and kicking his left leg up give A terrific power.

Fig. 10.4 Hip Lock

Stand Up with Inside Leg:

1. A must make three distinct moves at the same time: (a) bring the inside leg forward; (b) snap left elbow back and snug to the body; and (c) grasp his right hand with your right hand.
2. A then pivots on his feet.
3. A pulls B's right hand out and turns away from B.

Coaching points:

1. Must keep head up.
2. Must bring left leg forward for good base.

3. As you pivot you must move right knee off mat.

4. Be sure when you grasp B's right hand you have him by the fingers.

Fig. 10.5   Stand Up

Counters for reverses and escapes

11

A wrestler must know all the counters to the common methods of escapes and reverses if he is to maintain control over his opponent. It will be impossible to keep a tough opponent broken down at all times and that is why it is imperative that considerable time be spent in working on these most common counters. An adversary is dangerous as long as he can keep on all fours, because he can then force a wrestler to rely on these counters to keep his position of advantage.

The wrestler's best counter is to keep his opponent off balance and broken down in a prone position where he is unable to work reverses and escapes. In other words, he must keep his opponent busy trying to get out of breakdowns, rides, and pinning combinations.

COUNTER FOR SWITCH

Arm Breakdown:

1. As his opponent pivots out to switch, A slides his right arm down and grasps B's left thigh. At the same time he places his left arm around B's left hip.
2. A then pulls B's hip up into him taking away any leverage B might have.
3. A then grasps B's left wrist with his left hand and pulls it out from under him, forcing B to the mat.

Coaching points:

1. A must never let B get his hips away from him.
2. A must pull B's hips in tight to him.
3. A then breaks his arm down.

Why is it so important for a wrestler to know all the common counters for escapes and reverses?

COUNTER TO SHORT SET OUT

Snap Back and Head Lock:

1. Hook him under both arm pits as he scoots out. When he leans back into you snap him back.
2. When you have B back, switch your left arm from an under hook to a over hook. Then put your right arm around B's neck and lock hands.
3. Move your body to a 45-degree angle and spread your legs.

Coaching points:

1. To set up B if he doesn't scoot out, shove him forward and when you feel B pushing back into you, snap him back.

Fig. 11.1   Counter for Switch: Arm Breakdown

2. To change from under hook to over hook, put your head in B's left arm at elbow; this will prevent B from getting his arm free.
3. Once B is head locked, clasp it tight and get your arm out from B's shoulder.

COUNTER TO WING LOCK

Cross Over:

1. As B starts a wing lock to roll his opponent, A drops his head into B's left side to stop the initial move.
2. B continues to apply pressure to roll A. Then A crosses over B and goes into an over and under ride.

Coaching points:

1. The key point in countering this roll is the placing of A's head on B's left hip.

2. Then let B take you over, but you must keep your balance and land on both knees.

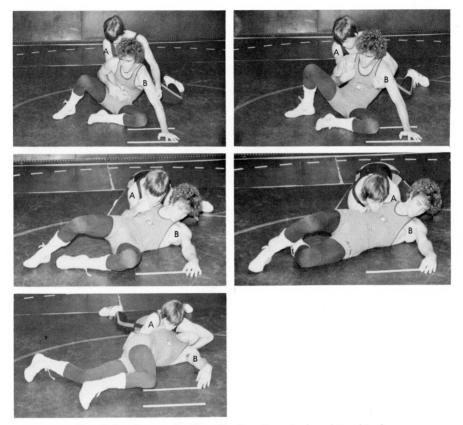

Fig. 11.2   Counter for Short Set Out: Snap Back and Head Lock

Fig. 11.3   Counter for Wing Lock: Cross Over

COUNTER TO HIP LOCK

Snap Arm Out:

1. B has A in a hip lock position. A must be sure he keeps B's left leg hooked with his own right leg and keep his knees spread apart.
2. A quickly brings his right arm back across B's buttock.
3. He snaps his arm forward hard and fast.

Fig. 11.4   Counter for Hip Lock: Snap Arm Out

4. Once A gets his arm free he brings it back quickly and grasps B around the waist.

Coaching points:

1. Must keep B's leg hooked.
2. Keep knees spread for a good base.
3. Arm must be brought back to B's hip.
4. Keep arm straight when snapping it out.

COUNTER TO STAND UP

Back of Knee Pick Up:

1. As B brings his inside leg up, A brings up his left leg for position to counter.

2. A catches B behind his left knee with his left arm. His right arm is across the back of B's waist.
3. As B comes on up, A picks B up with his left arm and throws him over to B's right, pivoting on his right knee as shown in the illustration.

Coaching points:

1. A must catch B quickly in the pit of the knee.
2. A must pivot on his right knee.
3. Let B do the work as he starts to stand up.
4. The most important thing is timing.

Fig. 11.5   Counter to Stand Up: Back of Knee Pick Up

Pinning combinations

12

Most coaches begin basic wrestling instruction by first teaching takedowns, breakdowns, rides, escapes, reverses, and, finally, pinning skills. Pins can be made in many different ways and all require the ability to control the opponent completely. At the beginning of a match when an opponent is strong and fresh, you should proceed cautiously until your opponent is worn down. The following are basic pinning holds that are fundamentally sound and can be used in a hard match.

Bar Arm and Half Nelson:

1. A breaks B down in a double bar arm ride with hands on B's left wrist and all his weight on B's armpit.
2. A crosses over B but keeps both hands on B's wrist.
3. A takes his right hand from B's wrist and places a half nelson on B's head.
4. A turns B in right angle to A's body and slides his right arm around B's neck to grasp B's left wrist again with his right hand.
5. A then forces B on his back, prying up on B's head with right arm. He places his right knee under B's head and straightens his left leg out for good balance.

Coaching points:

1. A must have full control of B.
2. Keep hands on B's wrist until you have cross over.
3. Place half nelson on back of head and not on neck.
4. Never turn B on his back until you have both hands on B's wrist. Pit of elbow should be in the back of B's neck.

When should the pinning combination be taught?

If an opponent is strong and fresh, how should you approach him?

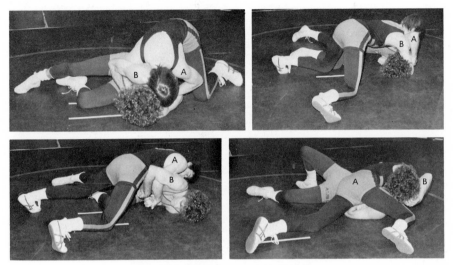

Fig. 12.1   Bar Arm and Half Nelson

5. Keep body perpendicular to B's body with knee against head.
6. Pry up on B's head.

Crotch and Half Nelson:

1. A shoots his left arm across under B's left armpit and grasps B's right arm just above elbow. At the same time he grasps B's right instep with his right hand.
2. He picks B up and puts him on his right side.
3. He then shifts his right arm from a back crotch to a front crotch. A then slides his left arm around B's neck for a half nelson and grasps his right armpit, being sure to keep body perpendicular to B's body.

Coaching points:

1. As soon as you have B on his side change your right arm from the instep to a front crotch. This is the key to this hold.
2. Grasp his armpit on half nelson or he will turn through.
3. Body must be kept perpendicular and legs spread.
4. When opponent turns toward you drive on your toe.
5. When he turns away flatten out.

Fig. 12.2   Crotch and Half Nelson

Chicken Wing and Half Nelson:

1.   A breaks B down in a double bar arm ride.
2.   He takes his left hand from B's left wrist and shoves it up under B's left

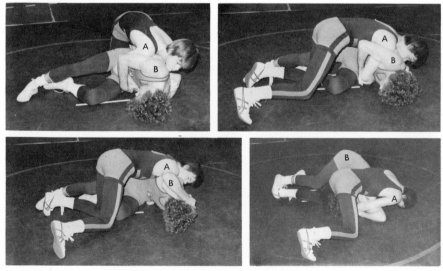

Fig. 12.3   Chicken Wing and Half Nelson

forearm until his left hand is on B's shoulder, using his biceps to press B's forearm tightly.

3. A crosses over to B's right side, being sure to keep a hold on B's left wrist with his hand and continuing to press B's left forearm tightly with his biceps.

4. A removes his right hand from B's left wrist and places a half nelson on B's neck, gradually turning him onto his shoulders.

5. On his knees A steps right leg across to straddle B's head; B is now standing on his head and shoulders. A must be sure his legs are well spread and buttock high to give him control.

Coaching points:

1. Once you cross over be sure you control the opponent's wrist and pinch his forearm with your biceps.

2. As you gradually turn your opponent pry up on his forearm with the chicken wing. This will stack him on his shoulders.

3. Keep knees well spread for good base and keep a high back.

Counters for pinning combinations

13

A wrestler may be exceptionally good on takedowns, breakdowns, and rides and still lose a match unless he can establish a good defense against these moves.

The four stages in preparing a defense against pin holds are:

1. The wrestler must be able to defend himself against breakdowns and rides as these are a prerequisite to pinning.
2. He must learn and develop the fundamental counters against half nelsons, chicken wings, arm locks, cradles, etc.
3. In this stage the defensive wrestler must set his opponent up by resisting pressure with everything he has and suddenly go with his opponent. The move generally causes the opponent to lose his good position on his opponent.
4. If none of the above strategy is successful and the opponent has tightened the vise on him until his shoulders are near the mat, there is one last resort for the defensive wrestler. He must then try bracing or rolling back and forth until the period is over.

COUNTER FOR BAR ARM AND HALF NELSON

Twist Bar Arm Free and Pull Half Nelson Off:

1. B has a double bar arm on A's left arm and is getting ready for a half nelson. A anticipates this and brings up his left knee so he can keep B from turning him. A has his head up.
2. As soon as B takes his right hand off of A's left wrist, A straightens his left arm and throws his left elbow into B's forearm to free his left arm.

Can you name the four stages in preparing a defense against pin holds?

B places a half nelson on A's head. A grasps B's right hand with his right hand.

3. A pulls B's right hand from his head to counter B's moves.

Coaching points:

1. A must keep his left knee up for good base.
2. Keep head up.
3. Snap left arm straight to free arm.
4. Once he has countered the move, snap his left leg back to prevent cradle.

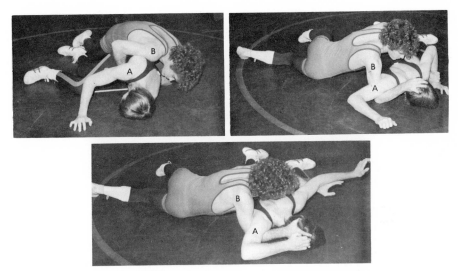

Fig. 13.1   Counter for Bar Arm and Half Nelson: Twist Arm Free and Pull Half Nelson Off

COUNTER FOR CROTCH AND HALF NELSON

Bridge Up:

1. When B puts A in a crotch and half nelson, A must turn into B by bridging up. Simultaneously A places his right hand on B's left thigh to prevent B from forcing A's shoulders to the mat, and places his left hand under B's chest.
2. A then snaps his chest away from B's chest to get space to shove his left

arm through. He may have to do this two or three times to get his arm completely through.

3. As A gets his left arm through, he turns completely onto his stomach, which counters B's move.

Coaching points:

1. A must keep off his far shoulder.
2. There must be a quick snap when moving chests apart so arm can get through.
3. Again, he must snap his legs straight to prevent a shift by his opponent to a cradle.

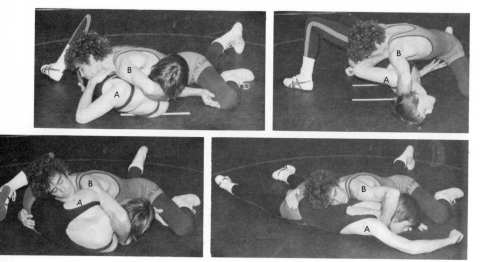

Fig. 13.2   Counter for Crotch and Half Nelson: Bridge Up

COUNTER FOR CHICKEN WING AND HALF NELSON

Pull Hand Off Neck:

1. A assumes the same position as for the counter to the bar arm and half nelson in fig. 13.3. A keeps head up and grabs B's right hand to keep it off of neck.

Coaching points:

1. Bring left leg up for good base.
2. Keep head up.

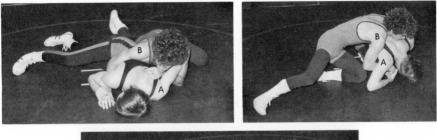

Fig. 13.3 Counter for Chicken Wing and Half Nelson: Pull Hand Off Neck

Training for wrestling

14

To be successful in wrestling, the athlete must be in superb physical condition. Every newcomer to this sport must realize that wrestling is strenuous. Every muscle in the body is put to use. A fine outcome of this is that no one group of muscles is overdeveloped to the exclusion of others.

Wrestling is not only a fine exercise. It is also a fasinating sport that challenges one's wit and both requires and develops agility, balance, endurance, flexibility, quickness, and strength.

The practice session must be well organized in order to make it most profitable and interesting. The athlete must know how to practice, the best methods of learning, how to warm up, and how to condition himself so that his progress can be speeded up.

HOW TO PRACTICE

1. Warm up for about five minutes, using calisthenics and conditioning exercises.
2. Receive instruction in fundamental skills and drill on these holds for ten minutes.
3. Practice competition using these skills for five minutes.
4. Review mistakes and drill on their corrections for five minutes.
5. Receive instructions on a new skill and drill for five minutes on it.
6. Practice competition on other areas (such as mat wrestling) for five minutes.
7. As you progress in wrestling, your instructor will let you wrestle more and drill less.

Why is wrestling such a fine body developer?

HOW TO LEARN

In order to get the most out of wrestling, you must discipline yourself mentally to the point where you will have the desire and the will to learn. You must pay strict attention to details so that you will develop sound skills. The following suggestions should help you to advance rapidly:

1. Warm up thoroughly, both mentally and physically, before practice.
2. Pay strict attention to each detail offered by the instructor.
3. Drill hard on each skill until it is mastered.
4. Work against a skilled opponent whenever possible.
5. Always give enough resistance in drills so that the hold feels good.
6. Do the drills correctly in every detail.
7. Use new skills in competitive practice.
8. Learn how to set up moves.
9. Speed up the drills as the hold becomes mastered in order to develop quickness and good reaction.
10. Put your all in each practice session so improvement will be much faster.
11. Study the results of each practice session for mistakes and weakness.
12. Work to improve errors and weaknesses.

Basic rules of wrestling

15

DESCRIPTION OF THE SPORT

The objective of wrestling in the United States is to win the match. This is accomplished either by pinning both shoulders of the opponent to the mat for a period of two seconds (in a high school match), or for one second (in a college match). If neither wrestler pins the other, either may still win on a decision by scoring more points than his opponent.

TIMING A WRESTLING MATCH

The time limit for college matches is eight minutes; three periods (1st period, two minutes—2nd and 3rd periods, three minutes each). In high school wrestling, the total time limit is six minutes, divided into three two-minute periods.

To start the match, the referee has both wrestlers come forward from their corners of the mat, receive instructions, shake hands, and then step to the circle. Then, while the wrestlers are still on their feet, the referee signals the start of the first period. When the match begins, the two wrestlers try to take one another to the mat by a takedown.

If at the end of the first period neither wrestler has scored a fall, the match is stopped and a coin is flipped to determine which wrestler then has the choice of top or bottom position for the beginning of the second period. Contestants begin from a starting position on the mat. The underneath wrestler tries to escape or reverse his opponent while the top wrestler attempts to ride and break his opponent down so he can secure a pin hold. If no fall occurs by the end of the second period, time is called. The third period begins with the other wrestler taking the starting position in reverse of that in which they started the second period.

STARTING POSITION ON THE MAT

The defensive wrestler assumes a position in the center of the mat facing away from the timer's table. Both his knees are on the mat and his hands must be at least twelve inches in front of his knees.

The offensive wrestler shall be on the right or left side of his opponent with one or both knees on the mat. His arm is held loosely around his opponent's waist with the palm of his hand on the other's navel. The offensive wrestler's other hand is placed on the back of his opponent's near elbow. His legs must not touch his opponent. Wrestling then begins with the referee's whistle.

POSITION OF ADVANTAGE

The "position of advantage" means simply that one wrestler has gained control over his opponent. To be awarded points for gaining "advantage," he must be on top and behind his opponent. The determining factor, however, is control. Under some conditions, it is possible for the man in control to be beside or even under his opponent.

OUT-OF-BOUNDS

When wrestlers go out-of-bounds, they are brought back to the center of the mat. When this occurs if neither wrestler has the advantage both start on their feet in neutral position. If one contestant has the advantage, he is placed in the starting postion on the mat in the offensive position.

ILLEGAL HOLDS

The beginning wrestler should always learn the illegal and potentially dangerous holds first. This is a safety measure. Knowledge of these holds will give him some idea of how far he can go with leverages. He must know that the joints of the human body should not be forced beyond normal limits of movement. Nor can holds be used for punishment. Wrestling violations include:

Hammerlock—Arm forced up the back beyond a 90-degree angle.

Twisting Hammerlock—Arm forced up and away from the back.

Full Nelson—Arms placed under arms of opponent from the back and interlocked behind his neck or head.

Toe Hold—Pressure hold placed on the toes.

Strangle Hold—Any hold across the throat that cuts off breathing.

Front Head Lock—Hold on the head when face to face.

Finger Holds—Any hold involving pulling the thumb back and/or one, two, or three fingers.

Body Slam—Bringing an opponent to the mat with unnecessary roughness.

Twisting Knee Lock—Forcing the leg to the side, causing the knee to bend into a twisted position.

How does a wrestler gain the "position of advantage" over his opponent?

Potentially Dangerous Holds—Any hold used in any way that endangers life or limb.

Scoring System—A wrestling match is won either by a "fall" or a "decision." Following is the team scoring system for "dual" meets (i.e., meets between two schools or colleges):

FALL: Six points are scored towards team total by each contestant who wins by fall, default, forfeit, or disqualification.

DECISION: (12 or more points)—5 points; (8 to 11 points)—4 points; (by less than 8 points)—3 points.

DRAW: If the match ends in a tie, each team scores two points.

Following is the scoring system for individual matches:

Takedown	2 points
Reversal	2 points
Escape	1 point
Near Fall	2 or 3 points
Time Advantage	1 point

WEIGHT CLASSES

In wrestling, the participants are matched according to weight.

College weights are:	High School weights are:
118 pounds and under	98 pounds and under
126 pounds and under	105 pounds and under
134 pounds and under	112 pounds and under
142 pounds and under	119 pounds and under
150 pounds and under	126 pounds and under
158 pounds and under	132 pounds and under
167 pounds and under	138 pounds and under
177 pounds and under	145 pounds and under
190 pounds and under	155 pounds and under
H.W.—unlimited	167 pounds and under
	185 pounds and under
	H.W.—unlimited

Be sure to check your rule book on weight classification as these have changed from time to time.

Courtesies and strategy

16

The very nature of amateur wrestling symbolizes a high level of athletic honor. The eyes of the spectators, officials, and coaches are focused upon two athletes engaged in a contest. Being the center of attraction, watched by both friend and foe, wrestlers not only should but must conduct themselves in a sportsmanlike manner. The wrestling mat is the laboratory where youth actually practices good clean sportsmanship. Wrestling teaches the sort of sportsmanship that stands up under fire. In general, the accepted practices of good sportsmanship in wrestling are these:

1. Never use questionable holds or try to punish an opponent.
2. Always accept officials' decisions graciously.
3. Never lose your temper.
4. Always shake hands with your opponent after a match.
5. Be courteous to opponents and officials.
6. Give your opponent the benefit of the doubt.
7. Be gracious in winning or losing.
8. Be a gentleman at all times.

When preparing for a match, the wrestler should acquire a thorough knowledge of his opponent's tactics and characteristics and should prepare himself to counter his opponent's best moves. He should know his own and his opponent's condition—this is very important in preparing strategy.

The good wrestler concentrates his attack on his opponent's weak points. He forces the other man to wrestle his way. Let's assume that you are in a wrestling match and that you are on the short end of the score. What should your strategy be? First, keep a cool head; your opponent may get overconfident and careless. Then try to take advantage of his mistakes. Try to make

---

Can you name some of the accepted practices of good sportsmanship in wrestling?

---

him waste energy. Anticipate his maneuvers. Try to make him wrestle your way. Try to make your every move count.

The best strategy and skills will not do the wrestler any good if he is not conditioned for the match, however. Good conditioning comes even before strategy.

An alert, skillful opponent will always try to counter every move one makes. In fact, it's the constant attacking and counterattacking that makes a wrestling match the fascinating and exciting sport it is. To become a good wrestler, an athlete must spend considerable time mastering the basic skills and counters. These suggestions will help:

1.   To get in good condition, wrestle often.
2.   Develop a few skills well.
3.   Develop a thorough knowledge of leverages and learn the science behind every hold.
4.   Learn tactics that will depend on skills rather than on brute force.
5.   Base your strategy on a sound understanding of the sport.
6.   Wear your opponent down with your skills and the use of your weight.
7.   Learn to fake and set your opponent up, and learn to drive hard.
8.   When taking an opponent to the mat, land in a good position with your weight on him.
9.   Look for pinning opportunities after takedowns and reversals. These are the times your opponent is caught off balance.
10.   Immediately after a takedown tie your opponent up into a ride before he can start an offense.
11.   When your opponent scores a takedown or reversal, always land in a good position so you can start an offense.
12.   Always try to react more quickly than your opponent from the referee start, both offensively and defensively.
13.   Study your opponent's riding tactics; then try skillfully to outmaneuver him.
14.   When your opponent is about to get out of a ride, switch immediately to another ride before he can muster an offense.
15.   Never leave yourself open for pinning combinations; keep your head up.
16.   Always break an opponent down before applying a pin hold.
17.   Never get overanxious to pin an opponent when he is fresh and strong. Wear him down first.

The language of wrestling

17

Advancement Points: Points are scored for each match won in a tournament.

Behind: The starting position of advantage on the mat.

Breakdown: Flattening out an opponent in a prone position or on his side.

Bridge: To arch one's back and neck to prevent a fall.

Consolation matches: These matches determine third place and subsequent places in a tournament.

Cross Face: Placing the forearm across the side of the opponent's face and grasping the opponent's far arm just above the elbow.

Decision: If no fall has occurred during the match, the referee awards the match to the contestant who has scored the greater number of points.

Default: When one of the wrestlers cannot continue the match for any reason, a default is awarded.

Disqualification: A situation in which a contestant is banned from further participation because of flagrant misconduct.

Double Bar Arm: Two-hand grip on the opponent's wrist.

Drag: Grasping an opponent's upper arm and bringing him to the mat for a takedown.

Draw: When both contestants have scored the same number of points at the end of a match.

Drill: Bringing an opponent to the mat with force.

Escape: A maneuver by which the defensive wrestler eludes his opponent from underneath.

Fall: Holding both shoulders to the mat for a silent count of one second (in college) or two seconds (in high school).

Flagrant Misconduct: Striking an opponent or continuing unnecessary roughness.

Forfeit: Failing to appear for a match ready to wrestle.

Head Lever: Placing the head in the back of an opponent's armpit and using it as a lever.

Hold: Any grip taken on an opponent.

Illegal Hold: Any hold that is not allowed by the rules.

Inter-arm: The interlacing of arms to break a double bar hold.

Interlocking of Hands: The hands, fingers, or arms around his opponent's body or both legs by a wrestler in advantage position unless his opponent has all his weight supported entirely on his feet.

Near Fall: When the offensive wrestler has control of his opponent in a pinning situation.

Neutral Position: Neither wrestler has control.

Overtime: In tournament competition when the match ends in a tie in points, the contestants shall wrestle three extra periods of one minute each.

Pickup: Lifting any part of an opponent.

Pin: Pinning both shoulders to the mat—often referred to as a fall.

Pinning Combination: Any hold used that results in a fall.

Position of Advantage: Gaining control of an individual by takedown or reverse.

Potentially Dangerous Hold: Any hold used in a way that endangers life or limb.

Reversal: When the defensive wrestler comes from underneath and gains control of the opponent.

Ride: The act of maintaining control of an opponent.

Seeding: This is used when two or more outstanding wrestlers are in the same weight class. One is placed in the upper half and the other in the lower half of the bracket. If more are selected they are placed in the other quarter of the bracket.

Slam: Lifting an opponent off his feet and thrusting him to the mat.

Stalemate: When contestants are interlocked in a position from which neither can improve his position except in a pinning situation.

Stalling: The contestants must wrestle aggressively whether on the top, bottom, or neutral position throughout the match. If this is not carried out, it is stalling.

Starting Position: Defensive wrestler—requires the wrestler to be stationary on his hands and knees facing away from the timer's table, so both knees are on the mat in contact with the rear starting line and the heels of both hands on the mat in front of the forward starting line.

Superior Decision: If the winner's score exceeds the loser's score by ten or more points, it is a superior decision.

Takedown: When a wrestler brings his opponent to the mat from a standing position and gets control.

Tight Waist: A maneuver in which a wrestler has a tight grip around an opponent's waist.

Time Advantage: When a wrestler secures a position of advantage, he starts to accumulate time. He scores one point for a full minute or more of accumulated time.

Unnecessary Roughness: Any intentional act that endangers life or limb, or that which is used for punishment alone is considered to be unnecessary roughness.

Warning: This is used when a stalling penalty is preceded by a warning. Thereafter violations are penalized.

Weight Allowance: For most meets it is net weight. For tournaments or teams traveling, allowance may be one or two pounds over net weight depending on number of days.

Wing: A maneuver used when opponent's arm is around your waist; it involves holding his wrist in tight and rolling your opponent.

Appendix: Questions and answers

COMPLETION: Fill in the best answer.
1. Wrestling is one of those very ancient sports that may have begun in the combative sense of men struggling violently for (survival). (p. 1)
2. We know that wrestling was a highly developed sport at the time of the ancient Egyptians and (Greeks). (p. 1)
3. What work of these ancient people indicated that they probably knew at least as many wrestling holds and stratagems as we do? (Art) (p. 2)
4. The middle-eastern and western parts of the world evolved today's two best-known forms of wrestling, free style and (Greco-Roman). (p. 1)
5. Interestingly, some Oriental countries evolved "martial arts" or highly refined defensive and combative techniques such as Karate and (Judo). (p. 2)
6. American wrestlers are at a disadvantage in international competition because the scholastic and collegiate wrestling rules and procedures are considerably different from those of the (Olympics). (p. 2)
7. This book is about American free style wrestling and refers specifically to collegiate wrestling which in turn is very similar to (scholastic). (p. 2)
8. Who coached at Oklahoma State University for many years and is one of America's most famous coaches? (Gallagher) (p. 2)
9. It is important to know that professional "rassling" is not synonymous with (wrestling). (p. 2)
10. Wrestling fitness requires a combination of endurance, strength, and explosiveness, and must include the entire (body). (p. 4)
11. In many sports, such as track and swimming, the athlete competes against the constant resistance of air, water, or gravity; on the other hand, the wrestler is constantly having to adjust his body to his (opponent). (p. 4)
12. The determining factor in gaining advantage is (control). (p. 11)
13. Breakdowns and rides are the preliminary to securing a(n) (fall). (p. 34)
14. One should learn the offensive moves first and to execute them to a fair degree of proficiency before learning the (counter). (p. 42)
15. Bridge is used to arch one's back to prevent a (fall). (p. 60)
16. The best way to get in condition to wrestle is to (wrestle). (p. 64)
17. In wearing your opponent down, you should use skill, strength, and your (weight). (p. 69)

18. Always break an opponent down before applying a (pin hold). (p. 56)
19. Never leave yourself open for pinning combination; keep your (head up). (p. 69)
20. Do not use questionable (holds). (p. 67)

MATCH TEST: WRESTLING TERMS

(30) 1. Reversal (p. 72)

(37) 2. Fall (p. 71)

(34) 3. Takedowns (p. 72)

(26) 4. Escape (p. 71)

(21) 5. Time Advantage (p. 72)

(38) 6. Near Fall (p. 72)

(23) 7. Forfeit (p. 71)

(31) 8. Draw (p. 71)

(33) 9. Decision (p. 71)

(35) 10. Default (p. 71)

(39) 11. Disqualification (p. 71)

(32) 12. Breakdown (p. 71)

(29) 13. Stalemate (p. 72)

(36) 14. Neutral Position (p. 72)

(27) 15. Hold (p. 72)

(25) 16. Illegal Hold (p. 72)

(28) 17. Position of Advantage (p. 72)

(22) 18. Slam (p. 72)

(24) 19. Ride (p. 72)

21. When a wrestler secures a position of advantage, he starts to accumulate time.
22. Lifting an opponent off his feet, throwing him to the mat with force.
23. Failing to appear for a match ready to wrestle.
24. The act of maintaining control of an opponent.
25. Any hold which is not allowed by the rules.
26. A maneuver by which the defensive wrestler eludes his opponent from underneath.
27. Any grip taken on an opponent.
28. Gaining control of an individual by takedown or reverse.
29. When contestants are interlocked in a position from which neither can improve his position except in a pinning situation.
30. When the defensive wrestler comes from underneath and gains control over his opponent.
31. When both contestants have scored the same number of points at the end of a match.
32. Flattening out an opponent in a prone position or on his side.
33. If no fall has occurred during the match, the referee awards the match to the contestant who has scored the greater number of points.
34. When a wrestler brings his opponent to the mat from a standing position and gets control.
35. When one of the wrestlers cannot continue the match for any reason.
36. Neither wrestler has control.
37. Holding both shoulders to the mat for a silent count of one second (in college) or two seconds (in high school).
38. Holding both shoulders to the mat for less than one second (a silent count of "one thousand and") or holding one shoulder on the mat while the other is within an inch of the mat, for two seconds.

39. This is a situation in which a contestant is banned from further participation because of flagrant misconduct.

POINTS BETWEEN CONTESTANTS

40. Takedown	(2)	(p. 68)
41. Escape	(1)	(p. 68)
42. Reverse	(2)	(p. 68)
43. Time Advantage	(1)	(p. 68)
44. Near Fall	(2 or 3)	(p. 68)

POINTS BETWEEN TEAMS

45. Fall	(6)	(p. 68)
46. Draw	(2)	(p. 68)
47. Forfeit	(6)	(p. 68)
48. Decision	(3, 4, or 5)	(p. 68)
49. Default	(6)	(p. 68)

TRUE OR FALSE: Circle the correct answer.

t F 50. Any hold that endangers life or limb is considered legal. (pp. 68-69)
T f 51. A boy can only wrestle in one weight class during a meet. (p. 68)
T f 52. A pin at any time ends the match. (p. 66)
t F 53. A college wrestling match shall last nine minutes (three 3-minute periods). (p. 66)
t F 54. A nosebleed is classified as an injury.
t F 55. The minimum size of a wrestling mat is 20' x 20' or 25' circle. (p. 10)
T f 56. If a wrestler is accidentally injured and cannot continue the match within three minutes, he defaults to the other wrestler. (p. 71)
T f 57. If a wrestler is injured by an illegal hold and cannot continue the match, the injured wrestler wins the match and scores five points for his team in dual meets. (p. 12)
T f 58. If at the end of the first period neither wrestler has scored a fall, the match is stopped and a coin is flipped to determine which wrestler takes top or bottom at the beginning of the second period (in tournament match). (p. 66)
T f 59. In American wrestling, the joints of the body cannot be forced beyond the normal limits of movement. (p. 67)
t F 60. The full nelson is a legal hold. (p. 67)
t F 61. You may pull a wrestler's hands apart by pulling back three fingers. (p. 67)
T f 62. One of the determining factors in assuming a good stance is to have maneuverability. (p. 25)
t F 63. Most wrestlers assume the boxer stance while on their feet. (p. 64)
t F 64. In the open stance the wrestler comes to grips with his opponent. (p. 13)
t F 65. A wrestler should take long steps and slide his feet on the mat. (p. 13)
t F 66. A wrestler should always wrestle "flat-footed" while on his feet. (p. 13)
T f 67. The offensive wrestler's first objective after bringing his opponent to the mat is to flatten him out in a prone position. (p. 34)
T f 68. The underneath wrestler has four points of support very similar to a table. (p. 34)
t F 69. The best way to break the underneath wrestler down is to drive him at a 90 degree angle. (p. 34)
t F 70. Poise and balance can be taught to a wrestler. (pp. 34-35)

T f 71. In the starting position underneath, the knees should be spread the width of the shoulders. (p. 25)

T f 72. Counter wrestler does not make a move until his opponent initiates an offensive maneuver. (p. 25)

t F 73. Wrestling has the tendency to overdevelop one's muscles. (p. 64)

T f 74. When drilling with a partner, give enough resistance so the hold will feel good. (p. 65)

t F 75. Slow up the drills as the holds become mastered in order to develop quickness and reaction. (p. 65)

T f 76. Condition yourself gradually to wrestling. (p. 10)

t F 77. Always try to hurt your opponent so you can just get by with the rules. (p. 10)

T f 78. Don't cool off too quickly. (p. 11)

T f 79. Wrestling teaches the sort of sportsmanship that stands up under fire. (p. 69)

t F 80. Never give your opponent the benefit of the doubt. (p. 69)

T f 81. Always accept official's decision graciously. (p. 69)

t F 82. A wrestler should match his strength against a stronger opponent. (p. 13)

t F 83. A good wrestler concentrates his attack on his opponent's strong points. (p. 69)

T f 84. A wrestler should develop a thorough knowledge of leverages and learn the science behind every hold. (p. 70)

t F 85. Learn tactics that will depend on brute force. (p. 70)

T f 86. When taking an opponent to the mat, land in a good position with your weight on him. (p. 70)

T f 87. Always react more quickly from the starting position—both offensively and defensively. (p. 70)

t F 88. Always try to pin your opponent before breaking him down. (p. 70)

t F 89. You should always try to pin your opponent while he is fresh and strong. (p. 70)

t F 90. Cross face is placing of the forearm across the side of the opponent's hips and grasping the opponent's far ankle. (p. 71)

T f 91. A drill is bringing an opponent to the mat with force. (p. 71)

T f 92. In the starting position of the defensive wrestler, both knees must be on the mat and his hands must be at least 12 inches in front of the knees. (p. 67)

t F 93. When the wrestlers go out-of-bounds and one contestant has the advantage, they both start on their feet in neutral position. (p. 67)

t F 94. The hammerlock is a legal hold. (p. 67)

T f 95. A wrestler is allowed three minutes time out during a wrestling match for the same injury. (p. 10)

T f 96. The placing of the head in the back of an opponent's armpit and using it as a lever is referred to as a head lever. (p. 72)

t F 97. Not all moves in wrestling can be countered. (p. 25)

ANSWERS TO EVALUATION QUESTIONS

Page   Answer and Page Reference

2   By the time of the ancient Egyptians and Greeks wrestling was a highly developed sport. That is, it was competitive; it had definite objectives that set up the goals to be attained; it was controlled by strict rules that determined who "won" and who "lost"; and successful performance required "know-how" as well as appropriate physical prowess. (p. 1)

3   The National Wrestling Federation and the National American Athletic Union (NAAU) have been carrying on a number of tournaments using the International Wrestling Rules. (p. 3)

6   Both muscular and circulatory (heart and circulation) endurance are essential for wrestling fitness. Endurance refers to the length of time that you can continue an activity or number of repetitions. Muscular endurance, that is,

the endurance of a particular muscle or muscle group, is developed by persisting, by repeating the strength activity. Not lifting a weight once, but over and over again is an endurance exercise. Again, the overload principle applies. If you can do fifteen pushups this week, try for seventeen—or twenty—next.

Circulatory endurance, circulation to the whole body, is developed in the same way. Continue total-body, especially leg, exertions over longer and longer periods of time. Fast walking for distance, fast rope skipping, cross country running, and running up and down hills—are all effective means of building this type of endurance. This is what will see you through a long, hard match. (p. 5)

11   Safety and sanitation precautions:
Do not participate in wrestling without a physician's permission.
Be sure to warm up properly.
Condition yourself gradually to wrestling.
Do not use questionable holds.
Never try to hurt an opponent.
Keep fingernails trimmed.
Do not wear rings or other jewelry.
Do not wrestle close to walls, standards, or other objects.
Do not wrestle in an overcrowded area.
Wear proper equipment.
Do not wrestle if you have any infection.
Do not lounge around after a hard match. Keep moving.
Do not cool off too quickly. Put on a sweat suit or take a shower.
Keep all personal equipment clean.
Be sure mats are clean and disinfected. (pp. 10, 11)

13   The techniques that comprise the basic fundamental skills of wrestling are presented in this book. A mastery of these skills should be the goal of every beginner, since they will enable him to progress more rapidly. It is important that the wrestler have proper instruction and then make the correct application when trying to master these fundamentals. Since there is no one way to wrestle and because no two wrestlers are built exactly the same, each wrestler should be permitted to develop his own style. (p. 12)

14   Coaching points:
Must penetrate deep into opponent's legs.
Keep shoulders and knee perpendicular to the mat for good balance. (p. 15)

26   Sometimes a wrestler is referred to as a "counter wrestler." This means he prefers to wait until his opponent initiates an offensive maneuver. Then he counters. This type of wrestler is one who tries to take advantage of his opponent's mistakes. (p. 25)

32   The first occurs when he gets behind while he and his adversary are both on their feet. The second occurs when he has control on the mat and his opponent jumps to his feet while underneath. (p. 31)

35   The wrestler's first objective after bringing his opponent to the mat is to flatten him out in a prone position. By getting B in this position, A has accomplished a threefold objective: first, he has eliminated the possibility of B's escape by destroying his base; second, A has put B in a position where he can be pinned; and third, A has gained a chance to relax after shooting hard. (p. 34)

41   It is imperative that a wrestler know all the basic counters to arm and leg breakdowns. He must be able to maintain a good base to operate from and never allow his opponent an opportunity to get good leverage on his position. The best defense is to take the offense immediately.

When his arms and legs are tied up, he must know how to free them. Then
he must take the offense quickly, forcing his opponent on the defense   (p. 40)

46   Escaping from underneath position to the feet (one point), or better still,
reversing from underneath to top position (two points) are important wrestling techniques to learn. It requires a keen sense of balance, deception, and
timing to work out maneuvers from the underneath position. Keep in mind
the location of the opponent's legs and arms and learn to recognize immediately what reverses or escapes could be used most effectively in this position.   (p. 45)

52   A wrestler must know all the counters to the common methods of escapes
and reverses if he is to maintain control over his opponent. It will be impossible to keep a tough opponent broken down at all times and that is
why it is imperative that considerable time be spent in working on these
most common counters.   (p. 51)

57   Most coaches begin basic wrestling instruction by first teaching takedowns,
breakdowns, rides, escapes, reverses, and, finally, pinning skills. Pins can
be made in many different ways and all require the ability to control the
opponent completely. At the beginning of a match when an opponent is
strong and fresh, you should proceed cautiously until your opponent is worn
down.   (p. 56)

61   The four stages in preparing a defense against pin holds are:
The wrestler must be able to defend himself against breakdowns and rides
as these are a prerequisite to pinning.
He must learn and develop the fundamental counters against half nelsons,
chicken wings, arm locks, cradles, etc.
In this stage the defensive wrestler must set his opponent up by resisting
pressure with everything he has and suddenly go with his opponent. The
move generally causes the opponent to lose his good position on his opponent.
If none of the above strategy is successful and the opponent has tightened
the vise on him until his shoulders are near the mat, there is one last resort
for the defensive wrestler. He must then try bracing or rolling back and
forth until the period is over.   (p. 60)

65   Every muscle in the body is put to use.   (p. 64)

68   The "position of advantage" means simply that one wrestler has gained control over his opponent. To be awarded points for gaining "advantage," he
must be on top and behind his opponent. The determining factor, however,
is control. Under some conditions, it is possible for the man in control to
be beside or even under his opponent.   (p. 67)

70   Never use questionable holds or try to punish an opponent.
Always accept officials' decisions graciously.
Never lose your temper.
Always shake hands with your opponent after a match.
Be courteous to opponents and officials.
Give your opponent the benefit of the doubt.
Be gracious in winning or losing.
Be a gentleman at all times.   (p. 69)

Index